...chell Jeweller. at y.e Sign of y.e Dial

...y.e Royal Exchange London ——

...e Gold, Silver, Mother of Pearl, Tortoise-

...Trieezer Cases, Equipages, after the

...ives Forks & Spoons, Gold & Silver Chains,

...s. Necklaces, Purses, Travelling & other

...Knotts, Combs, Fans, Spectacles. Fine

...are. The best Snuff. & Hungary Water.

...oy at Reasonable Rates. &

...r Jewels.

...aller a l'Enseigne des Armes du Roy, et du

...res pasons et Vendons toute Sorte de Curiosites

...tuelle Agate, d'Ambre, d'Ivoire, &c. Comme

...re, ..elé a la nouvelle Mode, &c. Etuits

...une d'Or & d'Argent, Cordons pour les

...rs, Bourses. Etuits pour les Voyageurs

...ons, Nœux pour les Espées, Peignes,

...toutes Sortes d'Ouvrages d'Acier,

...eine d'Ongrie, toute Sorte de Quin-

...m Juste Prix.

...lles d'argent ou Joyaux

Silver Toys & Miniatures

Miranda Poliakoff

VICTORIA
& ALBERT
MUSEUM

Acknowledgements

I would like to thank for their help and advice: colleagues at the Victoria and Albert and Bethnal Green Museums; Mr. Gerald Taylor of the Ashmolean Museum, Oxford; The Prints and Drawings Dept, The British Museum, London; The Lord Chamberlain's Office; The Museum of Childhood, Edinburgh; Amanda Herries and Tessa Murdoch of the Museum of London; also, Elaine Barr, Nicholas Bernstein, Karel Citroen, Christine Darby, Mary Hillier, Jean Latham, Stuart McCabe and Jap Van der Bergh.

Photo Credits: Trustees of the British Museum, London (pls 1,31); Frans Hals Museum, Haarlem (pls 10,40); Garrards (pl 18); Norfolk Museums Service (pl 64); National Trust (pl 79); Royal Collection (pl 99).

Designed by Aitken Blakeley
Photography by Geoffrey Shakerley
Edited by Philippa Glanville
Printed and bound in the Netherlands
by Drukkerij de Lange/van Leer BV

ISBN 0-905209-94-X

Contents

Introduction   5

Dutch toys   19

English toys   31

Playthings or artefacts?   45

Further reading   48

Front cover
Cannon: Dutch Am. maker IS 18c. M.28-1941
L.71mm
Back cover
Basket: parcel-gilt. Dutch Am. 1786 Hendrik Duller
M.39-1941 W.61mm
Title page
Tea pot: Pieter van Somerwil I (1706-53) c.1730
M.55-1941 H.30mm

*Objects are captioned from left to right and from top
to bottom if in a group. Unless stated all objects are
silver, Dutch and English in their respective chapters.
Amsterdam is abbreviated to Am. and London to Lon.*

1742

Snuff

Marie Anne Viet & Thos. Mitchell Jeweller at ye Sign of ye Dial
& Kings Arms, on Cornhill near ye Royal Exchange LONDON
Make and Sell All Sorts of Curiosities, in Gold, Silver, Mother of Pearl, Tortoise
Shell, Agat, Amber, Ivory, &c. as Snuff Boxes, Tweezer Cases, Equipages, after the
Newest Fashion, Ready Chased &c. Cases of Knives Forks & Spoons Gold & Silver Chains,
Strings for Watches, Seals, Pendants, Rings, Necklaces & Purses, Travelling & other
Cases, Canes, Whips, Spurs, Fine Belts, Sword Knotts, Combs, Fans, Spectacles, Fine
Flowers, and all Sorts of Cutlers Wares. The best Snuff & Hungary Water.
All manner of Fine Dutch Toys at Reasonable Rates.
Money for Plate or Jewels.

Mar. Ann Viet et Thom. Mitchell Jouallier à l'Enseigne des Armes du Roy, et du
Cadran, proche la bourse Royale, dans Cornhill, à Londres faisons & Vendons toute Sorte de Curiosités
d'Or, d'Argent, à l'acre de Perle, d'Ecaille, Tortue, d'Agate, d'Ambre, d'Ivoire, &c. Comme
Tabatières, Estuits à Cure dents & Garniture, Cizelé à la nouvelle Mode, &c. Etuits
à Couteaux, fourchetes & Cuillières, des Chains d'Or & d'Argent, Cordons pour les
Montres, Cachets, Pendents, Bagues, Colliers, Bourses, Etuits pour les Voyageurs
& autres, Canes, Fouets, Esperons, Ceinturons, Noeux pour les Epées, Peignes,
Eventailles, Lunettes, de belles Fleurs, & toutes Sortes d'Ouvrages d'Acier,
de bon Tabac en Poudre, Eau de la Reine d'Ongrie, toute Sorte de Quin-
quaillerie d'Allemagne, le tout à un Juste Prix.
Monnoye pour les Vaisselles d'argent ou Joyaux

Hanis Santo Scul Londin

Introduction

Model or miniature work in metal has been made since ancient times; miniature bronze utensils have been found in Egypt and Roman iron toys in Britain, all probably votive offerings. From the mid-seventeenth century a large number of tiny silver objects were produced in the Netherlands and later in England. The Victoria and Albert Museum is fortunate in possessing a large collection of these 'toys'.

The term toy at this time included any knick-knack or fashionable trinket, as well as a child's plaything. Silver toys copied the exact details and proportions of normal-sized pieces. They occur in an exuberant variety of subject and size ranging from domestic utensils to elaborate furniture. Dutch toys also imitate objects that would not normally have been made of silver (pls 2,32). Figures and models were also produced (pl 43). Several explanations of these objects have been tendered; that they were part of the furnishings of dolls' houses, that they were trade samples made in miniature for convenience and security, that they were practice pieces for apprentices, that they were a fashionable novelty for adults to collect or that they were simply the playthings of rich children.

Modelling in silver was not a new phenomenon in Europe. Figures on church silver, for example saints on processional crosses, and on secular plate such as the finials of cups, had been made since the Middle Ages, drawing on classical tradition. Large salts became increasingly fashionable in the fifteenth and sixteenth centuries especially in the form of ships, some of which had crews composed of individual detachable figures. An example is the Burghley Nef of 1527 in this museum.

Silver playthings were made for royal children; although none have survived, their existence is well documented. In 1571 the daughter of Henry II of France commissioned Pierre Hottman, a Paris goldsmith, to produce a doll's house to include a set of household utensils 'such as are made in Paris', as a gift for a child of the Duchess of Bavaria. Military toys, however, were considered more suitable for future kings, 'I have been to the Arsenal, Papa. M de Rosney showed it me full of beautiful arms . . . and he gave me some sweetmeats and a little silver cannon.' (Journal of Jean Heroard quoting the Dauphin, 1606). Another gift received by Louis XIII (1601-1643) as a child was an army of three hundred soldiers made by Nicholas Rogier. In 1650 this army was

2

3

augmented for the future Louis XIV (1638-1715) with figures modelled by Chassel and cast by Merlin. His own son was in turn equally spoilt. In 1661 Colbert ordered a hundred silver figurines from Wolrab in Nuremberg, to be incorporated into an automaton by Hautsch which became one of the wonders of the French court. These toys were supposed to give the young princes practice in military manoeuvres. Louis XIV melted most of them down to pay for his wars.

The Netherlands at this time was a successful trading nation based on the power and wealth of the leading merchants of Amsterdam and the Hague. Although they would have scorned the extravagance of the French court, miniature silver appeared in the Netherlands in the mid-seventeenth century when the Dutch seaborne empire had reached its peak. The Spanish had been repelled from Dutch territories at home and the Portuguese ousted from the control of the valuable spice trade with the Moluccas by the Dutch East India Company. For the past century large quantities of silver had been flowing into Europe from Spanish South America, making it available on a previously unparalleled scale. The Netherlands had entered on a period of stable government and their merchants settled down to an age of quietly conspicuous consumption.

This sudden popularisation of miniature silver coincided with a fashion for the dolls' house. The dolls' house was not a Dutch invention.

4

3
Fork: Dutch unmarked mid 18c. M.144-1941 L.44mm; Knife: Dutch Am. 1727-42 maker VS M.148-1941 L.64mm; Spoon: (1 of 4) Dutch unmarked mid 18c. M.145a-1941 L.51mm
4
Pair of dishes: Dutch 18c. Pieter Somerwil II M.138+a-1941 W.36mm; Dish: Dutch unmarked 18c. M.135-1941 W.38mm
5
Set of table spoons: Dutch unmarked early 18c. M.143a-g L.64mm
6
Sconce: Dutch or German 18c. M.128-1941 H.71mm
7
Candlestick (1 of pair): Dutch unmarked Late 17c. M.76-1941 H.44mm
8
Coffee pot: Dutch Am. 1717-33 M.53-1941 H.64mm

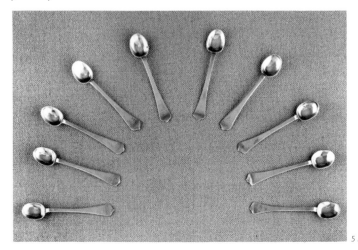

5

The earliest dolls' house known, of which nothing but an inventory now remains, was made in Nuremberg in 1558 for Albrecht V of Bavaria. Although ordered originally for his daughter, the dolls' house was placed in his art collection, perhaps the most suitable place for a miniature palace which certainly contained silver. About fifty years later, humbler versions were made exactly imitating contemporary German vernacular architecture and domestic interiors. The proportion of silver to pewter and brass would depend on the social status and means of the householder. As Christoph Weigel wrote in 1698 'The materials of which these dolls and playthings are made are in part silver and are fashioned by gold and silversmiths . . . Indeed there is scarce a trade in which that which usually is made big may not often be seen copied on a small scale as a toy for playing with'. It was here in Bavaria that the 'Nuremberg kitchen' developed; a single room fitted out with every necessary utensil and implement, usually made of pewter. The Hapsburgs possessed one with gold utensils.

Whatever the material, the purpose of both kitchen and dolls' house was educational. Indeed, in 1631 a grown woman, Anne Köferlin assembled a dolls' house and published an explanatory leaflet reiterating the value to the future housewife of such toys. Similarly, Paul von Stetten wrote in 1765 of an earlier age, 'Concerning the training of maidens, I must make reference to to the playthings many of them played with until they were brides, namely the so-called Baby Houses'. Some women retained these playthings after marriage; a Frau Negges in Augsburg spent so much on her dolls' house that she 'did hurt to her estate'. In the early eighteenth century the Duchess of Schwarzenburg created 'Mon Plaisir'; a hundred dolls' rooms representing daily life at court. This strange confusion of playthings for both adult and child will be encountered when examining the silver itself. Few pieces of German miniature silver survive outside these houses and it seems that they were made for this purpose alone (pl 29).

In the Netherlands the dolls' house was very different, lacking an architectural exterior. Such houses usually took the form of cabinets on

9

high stands, with the rooms displayed behind conventional cupboard doors. They seem to have developed from the cabinets of curiosities fashionable throughout Europe in the early seventeenth century in which were displayed rare curios; a surviving example is that of John Evelyn in the Geffrye Museum, London. These houses were equipped with miniature paintings, tapestries, glass, furniture and porcelain as well as silver (pl 10). They were in fact exact replicas of the fashionable interiors of the period. One well-known example, the house of Petronella

10

Oortman in the Rijksmuseum, (c.1690), even has silver displayed in the cupboards exactly as a Dutch bride would show her dowry. The luxury alone of these houses suggests that in the Netherlands at least they were intended for the amusement of wealthy adults (pl 40).

The quantity of toys being produced far exceeded that necessary to furnish these houses. During the course of the eighteenth century thousands of objects were produced in Amsterdam and the names of at least five specialist makers are known; the most prolific were Arnoldus van Geffen and Frederick van Strant. The fashion for dolls' house silver and the existence of these makers refutes the argument that silver miniatures were invariably trade samples or apprentice pieces; no one would want a silver sample of a frying pan or trivet normally made in iron. There are no contemporary references to work of this type and it is unlikely that whole services should be made when one piece would have sufficed. It is clear from English trade cards of the mid-eighteenth century (pl 1) that 'Dutch toys' were being exported to London and Paris. Several Dutch items in the V&A's collection have French import marks. The fashion amongst adults for collecting and displaying these larger pieces of miniature silver, combined with the export trade, could well have maintained so many specialists.

Whether described as 'Dutch toys' or not, it is certain that miniature silver reached England from the Netherlands. Cultural and trading links between the two nations were strengthened by Charles II's sojourn in the Hague during his exile. Silver was fashionable at the Restoration court and was used for many purposes, including furniture. Nell Gwynn's silver bed, made by John Cooqus in 1674, no longer extant, is the most celebrated example. The aristocracy and new merchant classes, keen to display their wealth, vied in the acquisition of curios and trifles or 'toys'. Between 1670 and 1760 much miniature silver was produced in England. A natural assumption would be that it served the same market as in the Netherlands.

English miniature silver was more limited in range than Dutch, usually reproducing tea and tableware and occasionally furniture. The figures that are so typically Dutch were not imitated. Baby Houses appeared in England in the late seventeenth century, rather later than the earliest surviving hallmarked silver toy, a sweetmeat dish of 1653.

9
Foot warmer: Dutch 1893-1906 M.4-1941 D.30mm

10
'Puppenhuis' or dolls' house of Sara Rothé c.1740 Frans Hals Museum, Haarlem

11
Linen press: Dutch unmarked 18c. M.65-1941 H.89mm

12
Gridiron with fish: Dutch Haarlem maker unknown 18c. M.91-1941 L.91mm

13
Chafing dish, wooden handle: Dutch Am. 1745 Frederick van Strant M.101-1941 L.76mm

14

Although not as luxurious as their Dutch counterparts some houses have survived with their contemporary silver intact. The only example of a Dutch-type cabinet house (with plain cupboard doors) was given by Queen Anne to her god-daughter Ann Sharp between 1691-1700 (pl 64). Another early house, also given to a child, Elizabeth Westbrook, was made by the tradesmen of the Isle of Dogs as a gift in 1705. Family traditions connected with both these houses suggest that the silver was added later, despite the fact that some of it is contemporary. Jonathan Swift provides evidence in 'Gulliver's Travels' (1726) that these houses were furnished with silver: 'I had an entire set of silver dishes and plates . . . not much bigger than what I have seen of the same kind in a London toyshop for the furniture of a Baby House'. Swift does not, sadly, tell us who played with these houses, whether adult or child. Most early examples are both tall and fitted with locks, suggesting that they could not be touched without adult co-operation. In 1715 an entire doll's house was imported for a child from the Netherlands, whether because it was a superior product or easier to obtain will never be known. The royal interest in the miniature never seems to have waned. In 1750 Horace Walpole reported that Frederick, Prince of Wales (1707-1751) was building Baby-houses at Kew.

Trade cards of contemporary jewellers and 'toymen' do confirm that a large adult market for expensive novelties existed, especially in gold and silver, (pl 1). Miniatures in other materials were also made ranging from Chelsea smelling bottles to pewter watch cases. Amongst these tradesmen was Coles Child of London Bridge, who in the 1750s advertised 'All sorts of English and Dutch Toys'. It is only seldom as on John Sotro's card of 1750 that a juvenile market is identified: 'All sorts of Children's toys'. Swift's evidence thus becomes unique, for it is only through him that the connection between miniature silver, toy shops and Baby Houses can be sustained.

Coppersmiths and tinsmiths also supplied miniatures for Baby Houses. Miniature pewter has a long history in Europe and miniature furniture has been excavated in London dating from medieval times. Toy wine tasters were made in the fifteenth century and there are some sixteenth century plates in the Museum of London. Interestingly the boom in the pewter

15

toy industry coincided with the fashion for miniature silver and the development of Baby Houses. The trade card of Robert Piercey the pewterer (1750) depicts a girl with her mother in a shop gazing at a toy tea service on the counter.

Oriental miniature porcelain was also given to children; 'Mary met me at the door and made me follow her into the parlour to behold a complete set of young Nankeen china which she had just received from the Duchess of Portland . . . indeed they are very fine and pretty things – not quite so small as for Baby things, nor large enough for grown ladies' wrote Mrs. Delaney in the eighteenth century. Items too large for a dolls' house thus seem to have been given to children for play, Bethia Shrimpton of Boston considered her 'Silver Baby Things' to be of importance as she mentioned them in her will at the age of 32 in 1713.

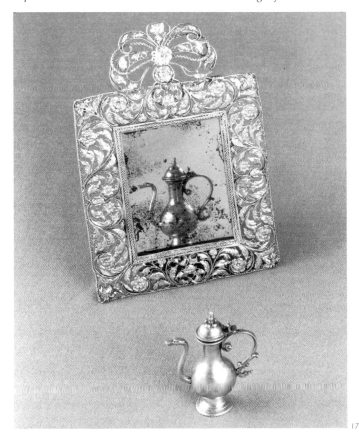

14
Family at tea: Dutch unmarked 18c. M.19-1941
H.46mm
15
Inkstand: English unmarked c.1685 M.226-1976
W.67mm
16
Cream jug: English unmarked c.1740 M134-1940
H.6?mm
17
Pier glass: ?Dutch unmarked c.1680. M.274-1976
H.160mm
Ewer: Dutch unmarked c.1700 M. 51-1941 H.58mm

17

Another possible use for miniature silver has been suggested. Furniture and porcelain have survived associated with early dolls such as Lord and Lady Clapham in the V&A (pl 21) and it is likely that silver was made in a larger size as accessories for such dolls. Lady Clapham has a miniature ring and Lord Clapham a sword. A sword of about 1730 in the museum's collection was probably also meant for a doll (pl 20). 'A Children's Party', painted by Hogarth in 1730 (pl 23) shows a silver teapot, tea-kettle and stand, and teaspoons all in proportion to the doll seated in its own armchair at a small table. A child also holds a small silver mirror against a tree. Silver too large for a Baby House was thus intended for play with dolls. The bigger pieces tend to be tea ware (pl 26), the child being expected to copy the fashionable adult ceremony of the time.

Adults in England also took an interest in dolls. A doll, dressed in the latest fashion, was sent over to London from Paris annually in the eighteenth century for dress-makers to copy. But adult fascination went beyond costume: 'However it is indubitably true that to make and dispose of dolls, such as children now alone are interested in, was a practice much in vogue a hundred years ago' (R. Chambers 1825). This interest might well have extended to miniature silver.

The dictates of fashion were important; 'As good be out of the world as out of the fashion' (Colly Cibber 1696). The vogue for adult dolls' houses and collections of miniature objects would seem to have spread from Germany to the Netherlands and thence to England. Art on such a scale could be afforded by a larger section of the population than just the court and dolls' houses made convenient display cabinets. In the Netherlands, where the fashion was most popular, the houses remained in this form. The silver itself reflected changes of style; after 1700 teapots

18
Entry in Lady Lombe's account 1739-40 Gentlemen's Ledger I of George Wickes (Garrards)
19
Tea urn: Dutch unmarked c.1760 M.35-1940 H.97mm
20
Sword and sheath: ?Dutch unmarked 18c. M.122-1941 L.83mm
21
Pair of dolls: English 'Lord and Lady Clapham' late 17c. T.846-1974

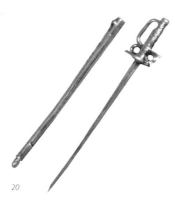

developed from pear-shaped to globular and by 1750 chocolate pots were rarely made due to the decline in popularity of the beverage.

After the 1750s, the quantity and quality of silver produced declined at the same time as Baby Houses became less opulent. It is probable that, as in Holland, silver toys served both the whim of adults and the delight of children until the change in taste left them entirely to the juvenile market. Children were becoming consumers in their own right and for the first time they were recognised as having special needs. John Newbery began to publish books especially for children in the 1740s and the dissected puzzle (the ancestor of the jigsaw) was invented in the 1760s. Baby Houses began to be filled with mass-produced German pewter and English ceramics and less silver is present just as porcelain competed with silver on the dining table of the great house itself.

22

Although the debate over the use of silver miniatures in England remains unresolved, more information is available about their makers. London, like Amsterdam, generated sufficient demand for specialist makers, the two most prolific being George Manjoy and David Clayton. It is clear that demand was high, for Clayton went so far as to import Dutch-made (and marked) toys and sell them under his own mark. It is surprising how little evidence survives concerning his customers. Occasional references in wills can be found but it is rare to come across records of transactions such as that of January 21st 1740, in the ledgers of the goldsmith George Wickes (pl 18).

The market in silver toys reached its peak at the same time as growth in the general retail trade. Contemporaries were not slow to note that shops were becoming increasingly lavish, with tempting displays;

'Farewell to Deards and all the toys which glitter in her shop,

Deluding traps to girls and boys, the warehouse of the Fop'

wrote Lady Wortley Montagu in 1736 of a shop in Bath, once again

23

bracketing the adult and juvenile market. Little evidence remains of direct sales from shops, and a bill of John de Crez to Earl Winterton in 1775 is a lucky survival (pl 31). This supports the theory that makers supplied retailers rather than marketed their wares themselves.

Miniature silver continued to be made in both England and the Netherlands throughout the nineteenth century. It was made for specific occasions; John Greenwell showed a miniature tea service at the Great Exhibition (1851) and silver accompanied later charitable exhibits, for example the Dutch doll Princess Daisy (1895). This baby doll, now in the Bethnal Green Museum, was made with a complete layette extended to include jewellery, cutlery and several silver utensils. Like most Dutch miniature silver produced in the nineteenth century these reproduced earlier styles. At the turn of the century, there was an astonishing revival. Firms sprang up in Schoonhoven in Holland and began turning

22
Vinaigrette: gold and silver gilt ?Dutch c.1800
M.64-1959 H.37mm

23
'A Children's Party' by William Hogarth c.1730
(Priv Coll)

24
Coffee pot: English c.1720 David Clayton M.48-1949
H.62mm

25
Brandy saucepan: English c.1740 John Hugh le Sage
M.248-1976 L.60mm

26
Tea-kettle and stand: Irish, Dublin c.1753 M.82 &
a-1939 H.173mm

24   25

26

15

27

28

29

out reproductions of eighteenth-century toys; much of this industrial production was exported to England. Meanwhile Birmingham once again had a 'toy' industry, as silver manufacturers started to make 'Georgian' and 'Queen Anne' services. These were even exported to Holland.

It is something of a puzzle why so little miniature silver was produced in the rest of the world. It is surely more than a coincidence that both England and the Netherlands produced such quantities in the eighteenth century at a time of growing prosperity and when there was a marked fashion for Baby Houses for grown women. An early eighteenth century Swiss dolls' house containing a covered dish of 1709 by Peter Biermann is in the Historisches Museum, Basle and miniature silver was certainly made in America. The earliest pieces (late seventeenth century) were probably brought or imported from England, but three early caudle cups including one attributed to John Coney (1656-1722) have survived. Miniature silver continued to be produced until about 1840. Both Mrs. Thorne and Mrs. Rubenstein, indefatigable collectors,

30

ransacked Europe for miniature silver for their miniature period rooms. Mrs. Thorne found some miniature silver in both France and Italy but little seems to have found its way into European collections. Other French objects are known, for example a coffee pot by Antoine Bouiller of 1775 in the Metropolitan Museum, New York and possibly a dish (pl 27) in the V&A's collection.

Once outside the era of the 'adult' dolls' house the dividing line between miniature silver as objects of virtue or as 'toys' becomes very blurred, indeed it would be hard to draw. Silver miniatures have for too long been neglected. Until more tangible evidence emerges argument over their use will continue. However it is important to appreciate them as an interesting phenomenon of their time and to study them for their own sake rather than as mere samples or replicas of adult-sized objects.

27
Dish and cover: parcel gilt ?French 18c. M.10 1941
W.75mm

28
Firegrate: English c.1735 ?David Clayton M.238-1976
H.100mm

29
Salt cellar: gilt, German late 17c. M.67a-1941
H.38mm

30
Tea pot: Dutch Am. 1758 ?Jan Borduur M.57-1941
H.38mm

31
Shop bill of John de Crez to Earl Winterton 1775
Courtesy of the Trustees of the British Museum

31

17

Dutch toys

33

34

'In my grandfather's house there was a small glass case entirely filled with everyday scenes from Dutch life during the eighteenth century. Since all these gadgets were made of silver, we children were never allowed to touch them. We could only look, but that was a good as playing with them' (Hendrik van Loon).

The museum owns about two hundred Dutch silver toys which form the bulk of its collection. They range in date from the late seventeenth century to the early twentieth century, but the majority belong to the most productive era, the first half of the eighteenth century. The earliest reference to Dutch silver toys is in a recently discovered inventory of 1635 which lists thirty-five items. They may be divided into three categories; those pieces bought as furniture and fittings for dolls' houses; the larger pieces meant either for play or adult collections; and lastly, the figure groups and models depicting Dutch life and purchased for display.

The Dutch toys (with a few exceptions) show much less variation in size than the English, most of the household pieces being sufficiently small for a dolls' house. A good example is the predominantly Dutch Lady Henriques collection at the Ashmolean museum. They were made both in silver and silver gilt. Surprisingly few in the V&A's collection are concerned with tea-drinking, many being imitations of kitchen utensils, lighting (pls 36-39) or furniture (pls 41,48). They were made in such great variety that it would be impossible to describe every type of object. Certainly the kitchen equipment (pl 32) would never have been found either in the

35

36

Dutch original nor in the English Baby House. Every detail was attended to, the kitchen being provided with its mouse-trap (pl 35), the lady of the house with her canary (pl 35) and the gentleman with his wine bottle and goblets (pls 33,34).

Although usually of cabinet form, approximately six feet high and with about nine rooms, the Dutch dolls' house was by no means standardized. The more magnificent examples in Dutch museums range from the beautifully decorated and informally arranged Utrecht house of 1680 to the contrived connoisseurship of the houses at the Frans Hals Museum, Haarlem (1740) and the Hague (1743). Both these later houses belonged to Sara Rothé, the wife of a rich Amsterdam merchant. The Haarlem house, originally made in about 1700 was bought by her in

36
Sanctuary lamp: unmarked 18c. M.46-1941 H.83mm
37
Pair of candlesticks: unmarked c.1740 M.284 & a-1976 H.70mm; Candlestick: 1753 Maker TE M.88-1939 H.46mm; Pair of candlesticks: unmarked early 18c. M.89 & a-1939 H.32mm; Snuffers and stand: unmarked 18c. M.75 & a-1941 H.62mm; Chamber candlestick: early 18c. ?Jan Bravert M.78-1941 L.79mm; Chamber candlestick: unmarked c.1700 M.91-1939 L.66mm
38
Candlestick (1 of pair): gilt Am. 1788 Johannes van Geffen M.86-1939 H.51mm
39
Snuffers and stand: gilt Am. 1755 Jan Borduur M.215-1939 H. (of both) 65mm
40
The 'Red Moire Room' Sara Rothe's House c. 1740 Frans Hals Museum, Haarlem

1740 when she was in her fifties (pl 10). She was sufficiently methodical to keep an inventory which reveals that she decorated and refitted the house with great attention both to current fashion and the relative proportions of all its contents. Disliking the silver fittings of the kitchen fireplace and determined to reproduce exactly the details of a normal house, she had them changed to iron. Similarly, miniature silver is displayed in the Red Moiré room (pl 40) in the Haarlem house in the same manner as it would be in the collector's room of a wealthy Dutch home. It was the custom to withdraw to such rooms after meals to admire the silver (or porcelain) and to play cards. A Swedish visitor in 1733 wrote of 'a large glass cabinet full of all kinds of silverwork, placed there to make a fine show and display'. As no such displays survive, this example provides invaluable evidence both of contemporary furnishings and styles in silver. It is also a useful guide to the average size of dolls'house silver as it was bought specifically for the house.

38

39

40

41

41
Secretaire: copper-gilt Am. ?Hendrik Duller
c.1780 M.1-1941 H.191mm Left: side-view
42
Tea-kettle: Am. 1748 Arnoldus van Geffen
M.56-1941 H.54mm
43
Lamplighter: Am. Frederick van Strant early 18c.
M.24-1941 H.89mm; Windmill: Am. 1753 Arnoldus
van Geffen M.31-1941 H.74mm; Cannon: Am.
Maker IS 18c. M.28-1941 L.71mm; Drummer: Am.
Frederick van Strant 18c. M.14-1941 H.38mm;
Pikeman: Am. Frederick van Strant c.1730
M.17-1941 H.76mm

*The larger pieces in the V&A collection are something of an
anomaly. The range in size of the candlesticks is shown in pl 37. There is
also a bigger snuffer and stand over two inches high which would not
have satisfied Sara Rothé and can only have been intended for play or
display. A painting by Hieronymus Lapis of the second half of the
eighteenth century shows a child playing with a toy tea service.
The very large gilt-copper secretaire is unusual (pl 41). It is beautifully
made and engraved but has some very crude decorative motifs, for
example the Roman head on the front. When contrasted with the
craftsmanship of the silver panels on the full-size seventeenth century
Dutch cabinet in the museum, it is clear that although it might content a
child or an uncritical adult, it would not impress a master*

goldsmith. Like the kitchen equipment, this secretaire is reproducing not a silver object but one of another material, in this case wood.

The best known of the Dutch toys appeared in the eighteenth century; a group of them is shown in pl 43. Those pieces depicting scenes of Dutch life remain static but some were made with movable parts, for example the windmill. They cover many aspects of life, military, domestic and outdoor activities being but a few. The museum even possesses a Nativity scene with the three kings and a star. Their popularity was tremendous, judging both by the number that have reached England and the fact that they are still being copied today.

42

43

In order to date and place Dutch miniature silver it is necessary to master a system of hallmarking which was neither as comprehensive nor as strictly enforced as the English. By 1503 the Dutch goldsmith was obliged to punch his work with the mark of his town of residence and his own mark which could be a symbol or his initials. In Amsterdam a date system evolved in the sixteenth century and in 1663 a lion mark guaranteeing the purity of the silver was added. However it is rare to find a fully-marked piece; a town mark and maker's mark are the most usual combination (pls 44,45). Identification of miniature silver is further hampered by nineteenth century reproductions of earlier styles, often bearing false marks. The similarity of many maker's marks is another problem, for example the marks of Carel Bogaert II and Pieter I Somerwil are both trees. Fortunately the later copies rarely reproduce the correct seventeenth century marks.

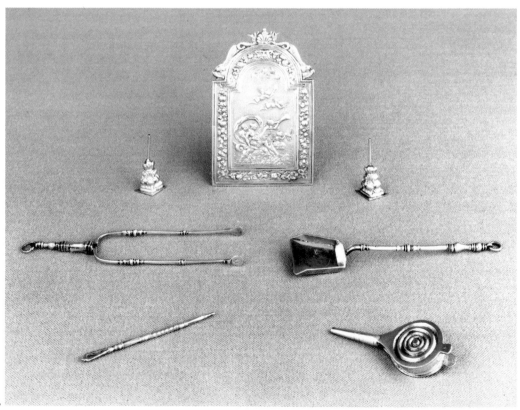

24

47

Despite these problems, many Dutch goldsmiths who made or specialised in the production of silver toys have been identified. Many are listed by Karel Citroen and in Victor Houart's 'Miniature Silver Toys'. Amsterdam was the centre of production although toys are known to have been made in most major towns including Haarlem, Utrecht and the Hague. In the mid-seventeenth century, the foremost makers were German immigrants, bringing with' them a tradition of making miniatures for dolls' houses like the Stromer house of 1639 in the Germanisches National Museum, Nuremberg. Boele Rijnhart was one of these goldsmiths who produced miniature silver in Amsterdam at this time. He made snake cups like the examples in the museum's collection (pl 54). Many of these early items are not copies of large pieces but

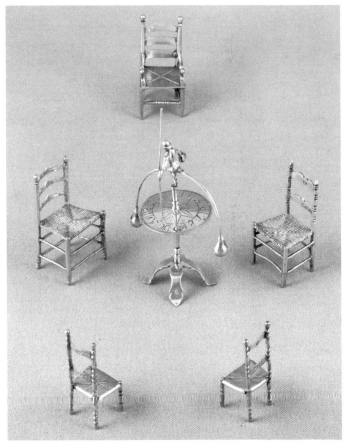

44
Am. for 1745 maker's mark of Frederick van Strant
45
Am. for 1748 maker's mark of Arnoldus van Geffen. There are several variations of this mark
46
Fire back: Am. maker FS early 18c. 293-1854 H.95mm; Pair of fire dogs: unmarked 18c. M.155 & a-1941 H.38mm; Fire-tongs: Haarlem 18c. M.87-1941 L.121mm; Fire shovel: Am. 1768 Pieter Somerwil II M.83-1941 L.114mm; Poker: unmarked 18c. M.125-1941 L.70mm; Bellows: Am. 1738 Frederick van Strant II M.103-1941 L.64mm
47
Tea kettle: Haarlem late 17c. M.95-1939 H.51mm
48
Armchair: 19c. M.118a-1941 H.64mm; Chair: maker WW 18c. M.114-1941 H.57mm; Chair: Utrecht 1736 maker DE M.114a-1941 H.57mm; Gaming table with marker: Am. 1776 maker HD M.5-1941 H.121mm; Pair of chairs: maker unknown 18c. M.97 & a-1939 H.51mm

48

49

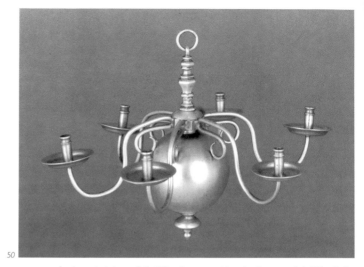

50

occur only in miniature (pl 49). An exception is the cup (pl 58) of the type known as 'Hansje in de kelder' (Hansel in the cellar) which, in a larger size, was given to pregnant women. Another specialist, Jan Breda (1665-1725) married Rijnhart's daughter and their daughter in turn registered a mark in 1725.

Dynasties of miniature makers were not unusual and the so-called 'Golden Age' in Amsterdam (1725-55) was dominated by three great families; the van Somerwils, van Strants and van Geffens. All three were established at the beginning of the century and specialised from the start; Pieter van Somerwil even advertised his wares in the newspapers. The three van Strant brothers came originally from Hanover and settled in Amsterdam. The museum has a day bed (pl 56) by Willem and a

49
Cup: marks indecipherable early 18c. M.68-1941 H.38mm
50
Chandelier: Am. 1747 Arnoldus van Geffen M.71-1941 W.105mm
51
Coach and horses: Am. 1787 Johannes van Geffen M.7-1941 L.108mm
52
Tea-urn: gilt Am. 1760 Hendrik Duller M.60-1941 H.64mm
53
Chocolate-pot with spoon: gilt Am. c.1760 Hendrik Duller M.59-1941 H.57mm
54
Snake-cup: gilt early 17c. M.101-1939 H.57mm; Brandy bowl: parcel-gilt 1750-1800 M.37-1941 L.64mm
Brandy bowl: gilt Maker ET early 19c. M.38-1941 L.64mm

51

chafing dish (pl 13) by his nephew Frederick who produced figures, such as lamplighters (pl 42), in the second quarter of the eighteenth century. The most prolific of all was Arnoldus van Geffen (who became a master in 1728) whose career spanned over forty years and who produced nothing but toys. His work is well represented in most collections, both in the Netherlands and overseas and is outstanding both in the range of objects made and its consistent quality. No object, whether a mundane butter dish (pl 55) or a complicated chandelier (pl 50), was considered too difficult to reproduce. The magnificent coach and horses (pl 51) is by his son, who registered a mark in 1766. In the second half of the eighteenth century other specialists still working included Hendrik Duller, maker of the silver gilt tea urn and chocolate pot (pl 52,53), and Carel Bogaert II, but although the quality of their work is high their output does not compare with that of their predecessors.

Miniature objects were certainly made in other parts of the Netherlands; for example the fire-tongs and kettle from Haarlem (pls 46,47), and the brandy bowl from Franeker (pl 57), all in the museum's collection. However the quantity produced was insignificant in comparison with Amsterdam where over forty goldsmiths made miniatures during the eighteenth century. Replicas in miniature of traditional Dutch objects such as the 'Hansje in de kelder' cups of the seventeenth century were not so fashionable in the eighteenth. These larger objects (pl 57) about two inches high gave way to the fashion for model figures and dolls' house silver which were produced (or at least have survived) in large quantities. It is clear from Sara Rothé's inventory that in the mid-eighteenth century miniature porcelain, ivory and silver were equally expensive; silver was not used as a cheap alternative. Many of the items in the museum's collection date from this time and reflect the changing styles in silver, beakers were replaced by goblets (pl 34), spherical tea pots appeared (pl 30) and there were fewer gilded pieces.

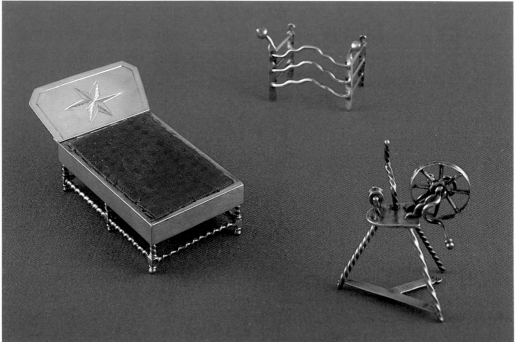

57

58

55
Butter dish: gilt Am. 1767 Arnoldus van Geffen
M.41-1941 H.48mm
56
Day-bed: Am. c.1730 Willem van Strant M.2-1941
L.70mm; Grate: unmarked 18c. M.79-1941
W.51mm; Spinning-wheel: Am. 18c. M.64-1941
H.95mm
57
Brandy bowl: Franeker mid 18c. M.36-1941
W.70mm
58
Cup 'Hansje in de kelder': Rotterdam c.17c.
285-1874 H.66mm
59
Chair: gilt 18c. unmarked M.98-1939 H.66mm

The earlier objects were often hand-raised from a flat, thin sheet of silver using a small hammer and were then chased and embossed, the smaller details being cast and applied by soldering (pl 58). Alternatively the whole object was cast in a mould and then finished by hand (pl 92). The second process explains the vast output of the van Geffens, for these moulds could be and were re-used. Thus old-fashioned styles were prolonged, making dating more difficult (pl 57). The sale of moulds between goldsmiths was not unknown. Towards the end of the eighteenth century hollow ware could be turned on lathes, thus speeding-up production. By the nineteenth century firms such as Niekerk of Schoonhoven were mass-producing miniatures in a town which had few goldsmiths a century earlier. Traditional figures predominate, although some versions show figures in nineteenth century dress, for example posing in front of a camera.

59

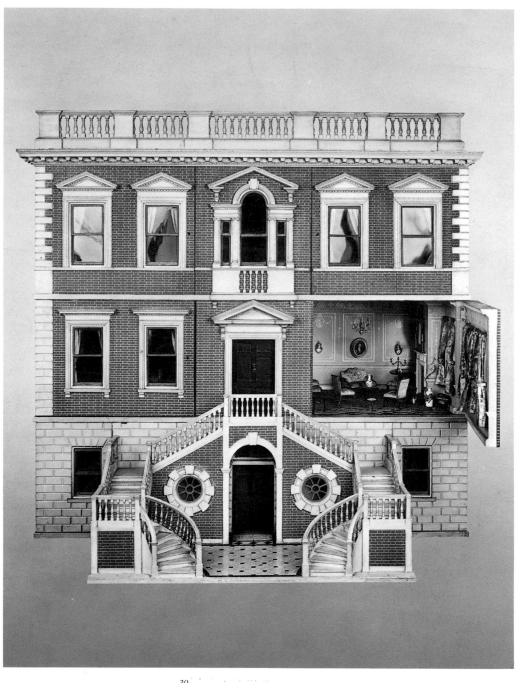

English toys

The Dutch fashion for miniature silver seems to have reached England in the 1650s. By the time of Queen Anne's accession in 1702, a considerable quantity was being produced. However, unlike their Dutch counterparts, the English goldsmiths made little after 1760 until the end of the nineteenth century. The eighty or so items in the museum's collection show a puzzling variety of size and finish but there is no attempt to imitate the Dutch genre figures nor to translate mundane household hardware into silver. The 'Dutch toys' advertised on trade cards in the 1750s (pl 1) were almost certainly of this type. The demand for novelties by adult collectors thus continued well after home production had ceased.

In England it is the earlier Baby Houses that have survived with plentiful collections of silver. These seem to have been added gradually rather than being specifically designed for the houses, hence the surprising disproportion of many of the pieces. In Ann Sharp's house (pl 64) there are eight pieces of silver ranging from a snuffers and tray of 1686 (76 mm) to a teapot of the 1720s (52 mm). Dutch houses of the same period contain considerably more silver. Silver, although expensive, was not as dear as the miniature Chinese porcelain or pierced Leeds cream-ware elsewhere in the house. The fifty items of silver in the Westbrook Baby House show a similar range of date, indeed it is hard to believe that they could all fit into its four rooms.

In the later Baby Houses such as the one at Uppark (c.1730, pl 79) and the Tate House in the Bethnal Green Museum (c.1760, pl 60) the silver is more in proportion. It is only the filigree box under the side table and the over-large casters in the Uppark dining room that suggest it is not a normal-sized room. The silver wall sconces and fire-back in the parlour are engraved with the family arms of the owner, Sarah Lethieullier. The silver, with a few exceptions, is contemporary with the house. By the 1760s the miniature silver is confined to fittings, for example the chandelier and mirrors in the Tate house or a single item such as the plate warmer at Nostell Priory. And yet the Baby House was becoming increasingly elaborate, the furniture at Nostell is supposed to have been designed by Chippendale; and the dining room walls are painted with rustic scenes.

60
The Tate Baby House: c.1760 Bethnal Green Museum (W.9-1930) H.1.6m
61
Coffee pot: c.1740 John Hugh Le Sage M.241-1976 H.81mm
62
Chocolate pot and molinet: c.1740 John Hugh Le Sage M.242-1976 H.80mm

Central Saint Martins College of Art & Design Library Southampton Row, London WC1B 4AP

63

As silver became scarcer in the Baby House, larger pieces were being made. Several coffee and tea-pots in the collection are twice the size of the Dutch wares and far too large for any house (pls 61-63). Whether for children, dolls or collectors, table and tea ware was beginning to predominate. Although it is tempting to believe that the largest piece in the collection (pl 85), a Newcastle tea-kettle 15 cm high, is a trade sample, it could still have been meant for nursery play as in the Hogarth painting (pl 78). A teapot, very similar to the one in the painting, is in the Museum collection (pl 77). The educative value of such play in training the future hostess was certainly realised by contemporaries.

64

65

66   67

68   69   70

71   72

63
Tea pot with wicker handle: Lon. 1765-6
John Delmestre M.80-1953 H.58mm
64
Ann Sharp's Baby House: 1691-1700 Priv Coll
(Norfolk Museums Service)
65
Wine taster: Lon 1690 Maker GM (George Manjoy)
847-1892 L.64mm
68
David Clayton's Britannia mark
69
Date-letter for Lon. 1709-10
72
Mark of John Hugh le Sage
73
Detail of molinet showing David Clayton's
post Britannia mark 848-1892
74
Detail of M.80-1953 Mark of John Delmestre
weight: over 2 troy ounces

There has been much confusion in the literature on toys over the identification of specialist makers of miniature silver in London. This is due partly to the similarity of maker's marks (several had the same initials, notably GM, MA and CL), and also to changes in the hallmarking laws during the period in which miniature silver was fashionable. Before 1697 a miniature should bear a full set of marks; the maker's mark (initial or symbol), the town mark (the leopard's head for London), the date letter and the sterling mark (a lion passant, pl 65). After 1697 when the Britannia standard containing a higher proportion of silver was made compulsory (in order to differentiate it from the currency), new marks both for London (a leopard's head erased, pl 66) and the standard (a figure of Britannia, pl 67), were introduced. London goldsmiths were obliged to register new marks, using the first two letters of their surname (pl 68). The date letter (pl 69) continued to be used. When the standard reverted to sterling in 1720, the makers changed their marks once again to initials. However it was possible, if the goldsmith so desired, to continue working in the Britannia standard.

Although the records before 1697 at Goldsmiths Hall have been destroyed, it has been possible to ascribe the GM mark found on many toys of this period to George Manjoy, due to the continuity of style with his later work (pl 70). Previously his mark was erroneously attributed to George Middleton, and his Britannia mark (pl 71) to Isaac Malyn. Tenuous links between the two were invented in order to account for the similarity of their work. Charles Oman in 1950 also ended a long-standing misattribution. By turning upside down the mark AC (which occurs on many toys of the 1720s) he revealed that it was not the mark of Augustine Courtauld as had been thought, but the post-

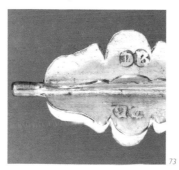

73   74

75

Britannia mark of David Clayton (pl 73). Moreover, he further proved that Clayton's Britannia mark (pl 68) had been wrongly ascribed to John Clifton. Thirty years later books and articles on the subject still refer to Courtauld as a maker of toys. Identification of the makers of miniature silver becomes increasingly difficult after 1739 when the sale of an unmarked piece of silver weighing less than 10dwt was sanctioned. Makers, not always exemplary in the past about marking their silver, did, however, continue to mark important work (pl 72).

Manjoy and Clayton were the two outstanding English miniature specialists, both producing high quality, carefully finished work. The earliest pieces by Manjoy date from 1684, and he rivalled the Dutch makers in the scope of his work which closely copied contemporary fashions in silver. His earlier pieces consist of beautifully chased cups and tankards (pls 75,76). He made a miniature punch bowl in 1687,

75
Mug: Lon. 1684 ?George Manjoy Engraved FD M.80-1939 H.38mm
76
Tankard and lid: unmarked c.1680 engraved with spurious arms M.191-1939 H.41mm; Tankard and lid: Lon. 1706 MA ?George Manjoy M.41-H.44mm; Mug: c.1740 John Hugh Le Sage M.249-1876 H.45mm; Tankard and lid: Lon. 1690 GM ?George Manjoy M.49-1949 H.41mm; Mug: c.1720 David Clayton M.46-1949 H.31mm
77
Teapot with wooden handle c.1740 John Hugh Le Sage M.243-1976 H.16mm
78
Detail of 'A Children's Party' by William Hogarth c.1730 (PrivColl)
79
The Dining Room, the Dolls' House Uppark c.1730 (Courtesy of the National Trust)

soon after the earliest large one known of 1680. He even executed a whisky still in 1688. In 1703 he made the only piece of English furniture in the collection, a cabinet in late Caroline style, long after the Stuart taste for silver furniture had passed (pl 98); it is thus highly unlikely to have been a sample produced for a cabinet maker.

80

Clayton is known to have worked from 1689 to at least 1730, and is considered to be the most prolific miniature specialist in England; indeed the museum possesses many examples of his work, including a rare plate warmer with a set of plates (pl 85) and a fireplace complete with fire-irons (pl 84). There are several miniature fireplaces in the collection. It is uncertain whether full-sized versions existed but silver sets of fire-irons and hearthboxes (Ham House) are known. Another maker well represented in the collection who also made adult sized objects is John Hugh Le Sage (pl 72), who made the large chocolate pot of about 1740 (pl 62), which still contains its stirrer or molinet, as does the example by Clayton (pl 73). These provide useful evidence since many adult pieces now lack their molinets, often through being used for coffee once the fashion for chocolate had ceased. Amongst other makers of items in the collection are Edward Medleycott responsible for the tea table (pl 82) and John Delmestre (pl 63). The only marked English piece in the collection imitating a non-silver object is the salt-box by James Slater (pl 81). The pair of canteens (pl 96) are both of about 1740. The smaller was certainly

81

82

83

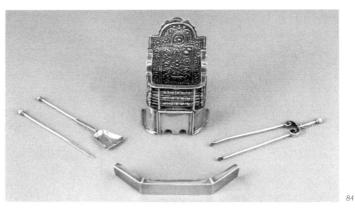

84

intended for a Baby House, a wooden knife box with similar brass cutlery is in the Westbrook House. The larger, although more elaborate, contains cutlery too crudely made to serve as samples and was probably made for a child.

80
Cruet frame with five vessels: c.1740 maker's mark IC M.254-1976 l 1 (tallest bottle) 51mm
81
Salt box: c.1730 James Slater M.240-1976 H.41mm
82
Tea table: c.1748 Edward Medleycott M.258-1976 H. 80mm; Tea pot: c 1740 John Hugh Le Sage M.243-1976 H 16mm; Tea caddy: c.1740 John Le Sage M.244-1976 H.39mm
Tea bowls and saucers: c.1740 John Hugh Le Sage M.252+a,f,g–1976 D. 39mm; Tea spoons (from set of six): unmarked c.1770 M.263+a–1976 L.55mm; Slop basin: c.1740 ?John Hugh Le Sage M.253-1976 D. 30mm; Sugar nips: c.1740 unmarked M.257-1976 L.55mm; Hot water jug and lid: c.1740 John Hugh Le Sage M.245-1976 H.46mm
83
Two-handled cup and cover: Maker IC M.255+a–1976 H. 50mm
84
Fire grate, fire shovel and poker: David Clayton c.1725 H.90mm; Fire-tongs and fender: unmarked ?David Clayton M.228q-d-1976 L 100mm L 95mm
85
Revolving plate-warmer: c.1730 David Clayton M.235-1976 H.90mm; Set of 18 dinner plates: c.1730 David Clayton M.233-q-1976 D.33mm

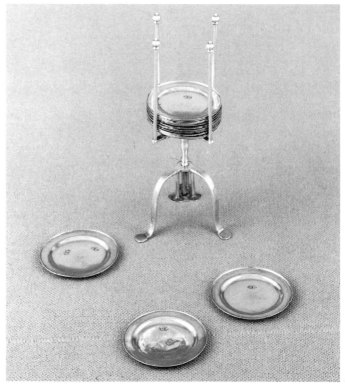

85

Several miniature articles are known with the mark of prominent goldsmiths who usually produced large-scale pieces, for example the de Lamerie coffee pot of 1728 in the Folger Collection or the James Schruder coffee service sold at Christies in 1972. However it is possible that these were made by specialists and then marked by the goldsmiths as retailers although the de Lamerie piece is unusually fine. The work of lesser miniature makers, especially after 1750 is very crude in comparison (pl 63), making it impossible to consider them as trade samples. The English goldsmiths used similar methods of production as the Dutch. The Queen Anne style adapted well to a reduced scale but Rococo ornament could not as easily be copied due to the obvious difficulties of technique and cost. A pair of magnificent cast candlesticks of c.1740 (pl 97) is an exception, possibly Huguenot

work. Manjoy and Clayton produced the greatest variety of items (pls 86,87). Later in the eighteenth century it is tea ware that predominates. Clayton's son registered a mark in 1736 but he seems to have made little. A few neo-classical miniatures are known such as the tea service by Samuel Massey of 1790. Although some miniature silver was produced in the provinces it is of little overall significance, the vast majority of work being made and sold in London. An exception is the Newcastle tea kettle (pl 90).

86
Pair of candlesticks: Lon. 1694 George Manjoy M.77+a–1939 H.51mm
87
Warming pan with wooden handle: c.1730 David Clayton M.237-1976 L.160mm; Chamber pot: c.1730 David Clayton M.230 1976 D.35mm; Chamber candlestick: unmarked c.1740 M.267-1976 D.55mm
88
Sauceboat: c.1740 John Hugh Le Sage M.246-1976; Sauceboat: c.1740 ?John Hugh Le Sage M.246a-1976 L. (of both) 65mm
89
Tea pot: David Clayton M.47-1949 H.43mm
90
Tea-kettle, lamp and stand: Newcastle c.1740 William Beilby and J. Bainbridge M.256-1976 H.155mm

91

92

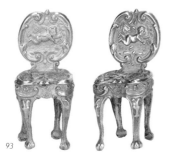

93

Periodic revivals of miniature making occurred in the nineteenth century but remarkably little has found its way into collections; this museum has a teapot of 1829 (pl 91) and the Ashmolean a toast rack of the same year by Rawlings and Summers of London. A tea service of this period was shown at the exhibition of Queen Mary's treasures held in 1954 in the V&A. When Jersey milk became popular in the latter part of the century miniature milk cans were produced as cream jugs. However the real impetus came in Edwardian times. Queen Alexandra revived the fashion for miniature silver and the price of antique miniatures escalated to such a degree that 'Queen Anne' and 'Georgian' reproductions were made by firms such as John Rose Ltd of Birmingham who are still using the same dies today (pl 94). Birmingham manufacturers also

91
Tea pot: interior gilt Birmingham 1829-30 Joseph Willmore M.5-1958 H.44mm
92
Salt: Lon. 1740 David Hennell M.95-1940 L.81mm; Salt: c.1730 David Clayton M.231-1976 L.28mm
93
Pair of chairs: Birmingham 1901 maker L & S (Priv coll) H.43mm
94
Tea service: unmarked 19c. BGM MISC. 211-1923 H. (of coffee pot) 40mm
95
Sugar nips: c.1740 maker IG. The only gilt English piece M.257a-1976 L.55mm
96
Shagreen canteen with 6 forks and 6 knives: unmarked c.1740 M.264-i-1976 H.38mm; Shagreen canteen with 6 spoons, knives and forks: c.1740 Key marked ID M.319-1940 H.89mm; Plate: c.1725 David Clayton M.233-1976 D.33mm

94

made some miniatures in contemporary styles (pl 93) and began to produce on such a scale that they were soon exporting to the Netherlands. It is interesting to compare the sale prices of 1904 with those of today:

1904 Miniature tea pot £8.10

Toy tea service £37.10

May 1984 kettle (David Clayton)................................. £620.00

February 1985 tea pot & stand (A. van Geffen) 1739 .... £300.00

97

Queen Mary continued the royal interest in miniatures and dolls' houses, presenting her own dolls' house to the Museum of London and being given in turn two famous houses; Titania's Palace (1922) and the house which was designed by Lutyens and presented by the nation in 1924. The latter is of greater interest as it contains silver as carefully worked as in the seventeenth century.

The house is equipped on a royal scale with a state dinner service for eighteen people, silver toilet sets in the bedrooms and even a strong room for the state regalia (pl 99). Miss Whiteside made the regalia and firms such as Barnard's and Garrard's supplied the silver. Sadly, as with the rest of the house, the designs are derivative. Some of these firms are still producing miniatures in the same Queen Anne and Georgian styles, as well as selling those imported from Holland and supplying small

97
Pair of candlesticks: ?English cast c.1750
M.269+a–1976 H.45mm
98
Cabinet: Lon. George Manjoy 1703-4 (Every drawer is marked) M.227-1976 H.90mm
99
The Strong Room, Queen Mary's Dolls' House 1924.
(By Gracious Permission of Her Majesty the Queen)
100
Cigarette lighter: silver with gold Lon 1977 M.2-1983
H.70mm; Pillbox: silver, gilt with gold Lon 1978
M.3-1983 H.12mm. Both made by Karel Bartosik

98

wooden rooms with fireplaces in which to display them. Perhaps this is the modern equivalent of a Baby House. Contemporary craftsmen are also producing miniatures of everyday objects in silver and gold, for example cameras and saxophones.

Playthings or artefacts?

There has been, and always will be, a market for the expensive novelty, whether miniature furniture or Fabergé egg. However, a whole range of objects was made during the eighteenth century when the fashion for miniature silver was at its height which, although tiny, have a function. These have often been included in collections of miniature silver.

Miniature drinking vessels are a good example. Small versions of communion cups were made for the use of the sick which were exact copies of the full sized object. Ralph Richardson of Chester made twelve such between 1721 and 1731. The snake cups and beakers of the Netherlands (pl 54), occurring only in miniature, were probably used as individual communion cups by the rich. The Russian 'charka' (pl 105) is an example of a small silver cup intended to hold a quantity of strong alcohol, in this case vodka; the Ashmolean collection contains some small Russian and Swedish cups. The German and English (pl 105) weigh on average just under a Troy ounce, and probably served the same purpose as did the early dish or 'taster' (foreground). The miniature porringer or two-handled cup typical of late Stuart England copies a larger object. This design of porringer is found in several graded sizes and it is impossible to determine whether the smallest are genuine miniatures or merely tiny measures. Contemporary references to dram cups occur but without mention of weight, or appearance. Cups of this type were made well into the next century. Miniature silver usually reflected the styles of larger silver; however if the porringer had become a novelty dram cup its unchanging shape is understandable.

Spoons present rather a different problem. Those in the Victoria and Albert Museum's collection range from three quarters to one and a half inches in length (pl 103). Small spoons accompanied snuff boxes, salts, mustard pots and etuis; snuff spoons are rarely found en suite with boxes but the few known are only one inch long. Spoons were also made on a reduced scale for babies and small children. It would be interesting to discover the size of the 'small tea spoons' advertised as lost in contemporary newspapers. In America in 1797 one Benjamin Morris bought 'Four Teu spoons children's Toy's' for seven shillings and sixpence from Joseph Richardson Jr., weighing less than two penny-

45

103

weights each. A spoon found on its own must therefore be treated with caution; when sets of six or more occur of a small size they must have been for dolls' houses or nursery play as in the Hogarth painting (pl 23). On the other hand, miniature silver with no apparent purpose could be put to use. The miniature fire-tongs (pl 84) are very similar to early sugar nips and may well have been thus employed.

Any small box poses a similar question. The Dutch 'Knottekistje' casket (pl 104) is a miniature version of the one used by the groom to buy his bride in a betrothal ceremony in Friesland. This could either be a novel form of box or intended merely as a child's toy. It was the fashion for ladies in seventeenth century England to make collections of small silver filigree objects, just as their Dutch counterparts acquired groups of figures. The Duchess of Lauderdale owned two hundred and fifty pieces of silver filigree in 1685. This would account both for their occasional presence in dolls' houses, as in the dining room at Uppark (pl 79) and

104

103
Spoons all English: Rat-tail c.1720 John Holland M.259-1976 L.82mm; (1 of 4) c.1760 ?Jasper Tookey M.262a-1976 L.56mm; (1 of 3) c.1760 Jasper Tookey M.261a-1976 L.73mm; (1 of 6) c.1770 unmarked M.263a-1976 L.31mm
104
Casket: Dutch 1893-1906 M.3-1941 L.53mm
105
Mug: English unmarked c.1710 engraved IR.MS M.180-1939 W.64mm; Cup: gilt South German (Augsburg) early 18c. Maker MB M.1077-1910 H.28mm; Cup: German parcel-gilt H.29mm 7244-1861; Two-handled cup: English Lon. 1664-5 maker SR M.297-1919 D.61mm; Vodka cup: Russian 1751 maker AG290-1902 D.48mm; Porringer: English Lon. 1761-2 John Moore M.163-1940 W.79mm; Porringer: English Lon. 1707 maker overstamped 809-1864 W.70mm; Two-handled dish: English mid-17c. unmarked 810-1864 W.53mm.

10.

in collections of miniature silver (pl 101). The chairs illustrated are considerably larger than the others in the museum's collection, making them unsuitable for dolls' houses. Filigree work is difficult to identify, and the examples in the museum's collection could be English, Dutch or German. In the Rosenborg collection, Copenhagen there is a miniature filigree cabinet containing minute replicas of the crown jewels of Denmark-Norway. It was made by Johannes Müller, Bergen, in 1736. The V&A collection also includes a miniature silver gridiron similar to an eighteenth century Dutch toy (pl 102) engraved with the words 'Drury Club 1826', perhaps the badge of a dining club.

Miniature utensils could have been used as scent flasks, for example the Dutch flask made from a carved nut (pl 107), or the Dutch chinoiserie tea caddy (pl 108), perhaps filled with the aid of miniature wine funnels.

Lastly there are the 'toys' in the true eighteenth century sense of trifles or novelties, produced in a vast range of form and material; the majority were made in Birmingham at the end of the eighteenth century causing it to be dubbed the 'toyshop of the world'. Some of these had a function, the gold tea table (pl 22) is an elaborate example of a vinaigrette (a container of aromatic vinegar to ward off smells). Dutch 'toys' in the collection include the backgammon board (pl 106) with chess and nine men's morris on its other sides. However, either the goldsmith had no knowledge of the games or it was never intended for use as insufficient room is allowed to position the counters correctly. The fish (pl 109) is a small container, identical to some English vinaigrettes. Also in the collection are various animals such as a silver lion and pendant charms ranging from a boot to a chisel, a fashion revived in the 1920s.

106
Games board (hinged) with 27 pieces and 2 dice.
Dutch 18c. mark unidentified M.124-1941 L.122mm
107
Flask. Dutch carved nut mounted in silver (with stopper) M.48-1941 H.53mm
108
Tea caddy: Dutch c.1730 Willem van Strant (Priv coll) H.45mm
109
Articulated fish: Dutch or German 18c. M.123-1941 L.70mm

109

Further reading

Miniature Silver: Books & Articles

Victor Houart: 'Miniature Silver Toys' Alpine Fine Arts, NY 1981

B. Hughes & Therle Hughes: 'Collecting Miniature Antiques' Heinemann 1973

Eric Delieb: 'Investing in Silver' Barrie & Rockiff 1967

Charles Oman: 'English Silver Toys' Apollo, Miscellany 1949

J. Banister: 'Silver Toys and Miniatures' Antique Collector Feb. 1975

J.D. Kernan: 'American Miniature Silver' Antiques December 1961

Hallmarks

Sir Charles James Jackson: 'English Goldsmiths and their Marks' (1964 reprint)

A. Grimwade: 'The London Goldsmiths, 1697-1837' 2nd ed. 1982

Karel Citroen: 'Amsterdam Silversmiths and their Marks' North Holland Publishing Co. 1975

Karel Citroen: 'Valse Zilvermarken in Nederland' 1977

Dolls' Houses

Vivian Greene: 'English Dolls' Houses' Batsford 1955

Flora Jacobs: 'A History of Dolls' Houses' Cassell & Co. 1954

Jean Latham: 'Dolls' Houses' A&C Black 1969

Collections to Visit: British Isles

Ashmolean Museum, Oxford (Reserve coll.)

Bethnal Green Museum, London. Also Dolls' Houses

Manchester City A.G. Assheton Bennett Collection

Museum of Childhood, Edinburgh

Museum of London (Reserve coll.) Also Dolls' Houses

Windsor Castle (Queen Mary's Dolls' House)

Collections to Visit: Netherlands

Rijksmuseum, Amsterdam

Frans Hals Museum, Haarlem

Collections to Visit: United States of America

Philadelphia Museum of Fine Arts, Boston Mass.

Art Institute, Chicago

Yale University Art Gallery

Márie Anne Viet & Thoˢ M[...]
—— & Kings Arms, on Cornhill n[...]
Make and Sell, All sorts of Curiositi[...]
Shell, Agat, Amber, Ivory, &c. as Snuff-Bo[...]
Newest Fashion Ready Chased &c. Cases of [...]
Strings for Watches, Seals, Pendants, R[...]
Cases, Canes, Whips, Spurs, Fine Belts, Sno[...]
Flowers, and all sorts of Cuttler[...]
All manner of Fine Dutc[...]
—— Money for Plat[...]

Mar: Ann Viet et Thom: Mitchell[...]
Cadran, proche la bourse Royale, dans Cornhill, a[...]
d'Or, d'Argent & Nacre de Perle, d'Écaille[...]
Tabatières, Estuits a Cure dents & Garn[...]
a Couteaux fourchetetes, & Cuillieres, des [...]
Montres, Cachets, Pendents, Bagues, Co[...]
& autres, Canes, Foüets, Esperons, Cein[...]
Evantailles, Lunettes, de belles Fleur[...]
de bon Tabac en Poudre, Eau de la[...]
-quaillerie d'Allemagne, le tout [...]
Monnoye pour les Vay[...]